Mr. Business
The Adventures of Little BK

Book 1: The First Day of School

Written by
B.K. Fulton

Illustrated by
Salaam Muhammad

www.soulidifly.com

Mr. Business Book 1

Welcome to the Mr. Business series!

Mr. Business is a dynamic, entertaining series of books that are steeped in life lessons that encourage children to be true to who they are.

Copyright © 2019 by BK Fulton

ISBN: 978-1-949929-06-5

Library of Congress Control Number: In Progress

All rights reserved. No part of this book may be reproduced in any manner whatsoever, stored in a retrieval system or transmitted in any form or by any means, electronic, mechanical, photocopying, recording, or otherwise without written permission from the publisher. For information regarding permission, write to Owl Publishing, LLC.

All Rights Reserved. Published by Owl Publishing, LLC.
150 Parkview Heights Road
Ephrata, PA 17522, www.owlpublishinghouse.com,
by arrangement with Soulidifly Productions.

Dedication

Thank you for choosing Mr. Business. This series is dedicated to all the kids out there who work smart and try their best every day at home and at school. The series is also dedicated to all the caring adults who help our young people to be excellent. Each day is a gift. What we do with that gift is our gift back to the planet. You are excellent by design.

Sincerely,

B.K. Fulton

"Wake up, Brian!
It's your first day of school!"

"Oh man," he thought, "the first day of third grade in a new school!"

He hoped it was going to be an exciting day.

"Don't call me Brian, mom," he said. He hated when she called him Brian. It usually meant he was in trouble! She handed him his glasses.

"Call me Keith, I like my middle name better. Keith is cool."

His mom frowned. "I named you Brian," she said. "So that's what I'm going to call you."

"A new school," he thought, smiling. "I'm going to tell everyone my name is Keith!"

A new school would mean a new start. And a new name! He was nervous about the first day of school. He did not know the kids in the neighborhood yet. Would they like him?

Plus, he was wearing those checkered pants and that funny hat with the flaps. Maybe he looked more like "Brian!"

The bus pulled up and he stepped on and sat down. A kid popped up from the seat behind him.

"Nice hat, new kid!" he laughed.

"Sit down, Grimes!" the bus driver yelled.

Yeah, Keith was in trouble. Grimes gave him the I'm-going-to-get-you-after-school look.

Keith ducked his head and adjusted his smart-guy glasses. He avoided Grimes all day.

Third grade was hard enough without checkered pants and glasses and a hat with flaps.

When the last bell rang, the race for the bus began.

If he got on the bus first, the bus driver could protect him and he could get a head start on the run home once the bus reached his stop.

Grimes gave him the mean-eye as soon as he got on the bus.

He got on a little late, but found a seat behind Keith so he could keep his eyes on him.

The bus rode along. Keith and Grimes did not say a word, but Keith could feel Grimes staring at him.

"I'm so happy I have on my fast shoes," Keith thought to himself.

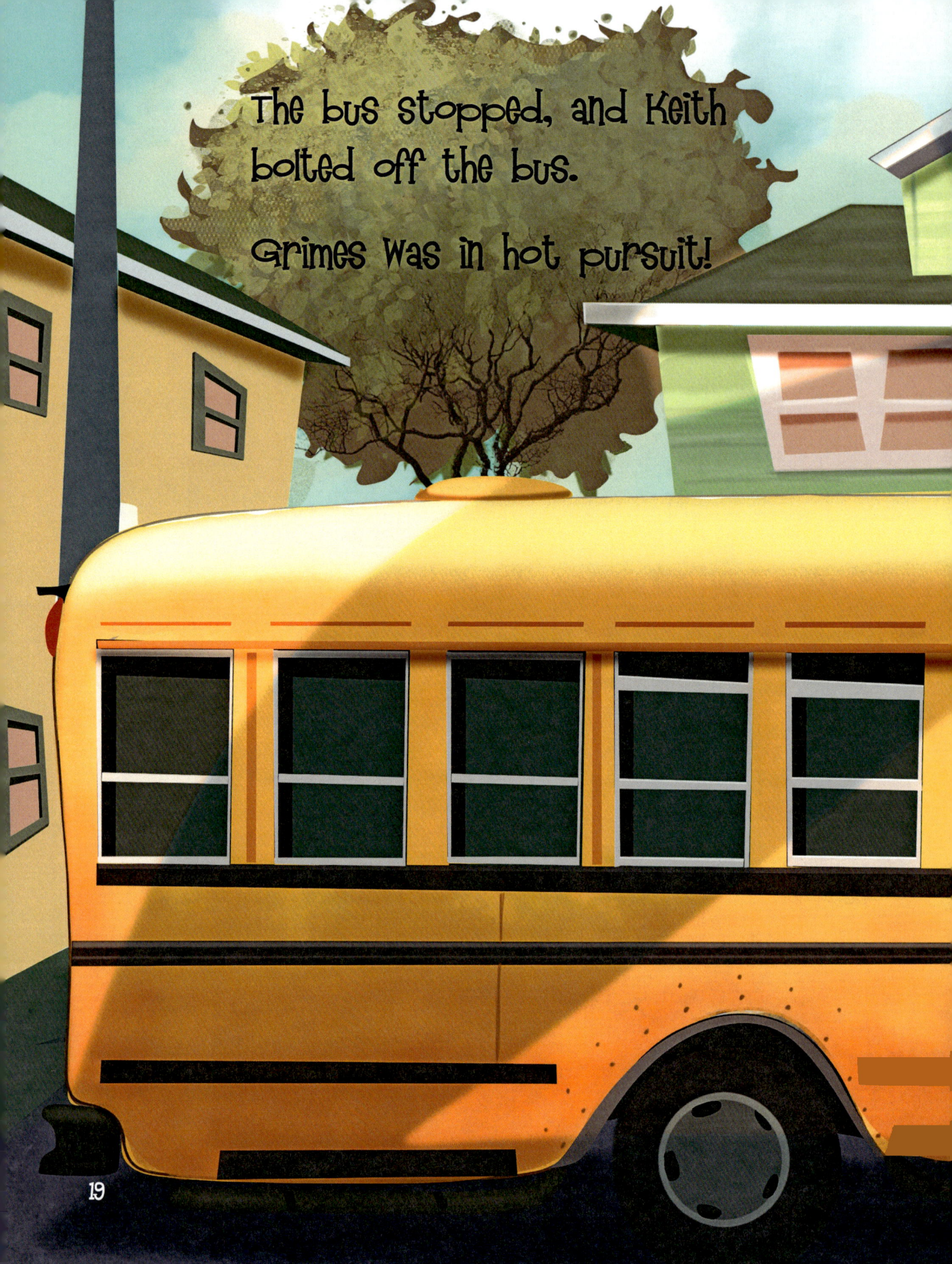
The bus stopped, and Keith bolted off the bus.

Grimes was in hot pursuit!

They ran past the bushes and the trees.
They ran past the big house on the corner.

They ran right up to Keith's house and kept going into his back yard.

Rusty, Keith's faithful dog, was in the back yard.

Keith ran straight to Rusty.

Grimes stopped all of a sudden when Rusty began to bark and growl a little.

Come on now," Keith yelled.
"Come and get me now!"

He smiled. Rusty had saved him.

Grimes turned and grinned, then said, "We have school tomorrow too . . ."

"Rusty will be waiting," Keith said.

Then he heard his Mom calling,
"Brian come inside. Time to do your homework."

Being called "Brian" was not so bad. Maybe he could be Brian and Keith? This was the beginning of "BK."

There was still more school and more to learn about the new neighborhood, but today was a good day for Little BK.

Mr. Business Journal

A good friend always has your back.

About the Author

BK Fulton is an author, filmmaker, philanthropist, and entrepreneur. BK was awarded a Computerworld Smithsonian International Technology Laureates Medal and his influential writings on technology are permanently archived at the Smithsonian Institute. He lives in Virginia with his wife, Jackie, where they raised twin boys. His series, Mr. Business, tells the story of his life growing up.

About the Illustrator

Salaam Muhammad is a self-taught artist who created his own unique style of art. He likes to focus on powerful, positive and impactful imagery because good art can change the world. Salaam was featured in the annual Harlem Fine Arts Festival, and lives near Philadelphia.

Made in United States
North Haven, CT
02 December 2021